Countries We Come From

Armenia

by Rachel Rose

Consultant: Marjorie Faulstich Orellana, PhD
Professor of Urban Schooling
University of California, Los Angeles

BEARPORT PUBLISHING

New York, New York

Credits

Cover, © Jacek Chabraszewski/Shutterstock and © efesenko/iStock; 3, © ruzanna/Shutterstock; 4, © By javarman/Shutterstock; 5, © Claudiad/Getty Images; 5T, © Mantvydas Drevinskas/Shutterstock; 7B, © M Sosnowska/Shutterstock; 8–9, © eFesenko/Shutterstock; 9, © Aram Atyan/Shutterstock; 10T, © IrinaK/Shutterstock; 10B, © Vladislav T. Jirousek/Shutterstock; 11, © PRILL/Shutterstock; 12, © Ruzanna/Shutterstock; 13T, © Nick Biemans/Shutterstock; 13B, © Vahan Abrahamyan/Shutterstock; 14, © LukaKikina/Shutterstock; 15T, © Ruslan Harutyunov/Shutterstock; 15B, © Gromwell/Shutterstock; 16, © Karen Faljyan/Shutterstock; 17, © Mikhail Pogosov/Shutterstock; 18, © Everett Historical/Shutterstock; 19, © GYG Studio/Shutterstock; 20–21, © Dinozzzaver/Shutterstock; 22, © MicheleB/Shutterstock; 23T, © minadezhda/Shutterstock; 23B, © Nomad_Soul/Shutterstock; 24, © Danita Delmont/Shutterstock; 25, © tunart/Getty Images; 26, © VahanN/Shutterstock; 27, © Aleksandra Mielcarek/Shutterstock; 28–29, © Artem Avetisyan/Shutterstock; 29T, © Pavel L Photo and Video/Shutterstock; 29B, © HERO TOWN/Shutterstock; 30T, © phamat123/Shutterstock; 30B, © Ikatiekk/Shutterstock; 31 (T to B), © Rosita So Image/Getty Images, © Mis fotos de viajes/Getty Images, © PRILL/Shutterstock, © GYG Studio/Shutterstock, © Aleksandar Milosavljevic/EyeEm/Getty Images, and © Luis Dafos/Getty Images; 32, © Blofeld of SPECTRE/Wikimedia.

Publisher: Kenn Goin
Senior Editor: Joyce Tavolacci
Creative Director: Spencer Brinker
Design: Debrah Kaiser
Photo Researcher: Book Buddy Media

Library of Congress Cataloging-in-Publication Data

Names: Rose, Rachel, 1968– author.
Title: Armenia / by Rachel Rose.
Description: New York, New York: Bearport Publishing, [2020] | Series:
   Countries we come from | Includes bibliographical references and index. |
Identifiers: LCCN 2019010072 (print) | LCCN 2019011117 (ebook) | ISBN
   9781642805826 (ebook) | ISBN 9781642805284 (library binding)
Subjects: LCSH: Armenia (Republic)—Juvenile literature.
Classification: LCC DK682.3 (ebook) | LCC DK682.3 .R67 2020 (print) | DDC
   947.56—dc23
LC record available at https://lccn.loc.gov/2019010072

For more information, write to Bearport Publishing Company, Inc., 45 West 21st Street, Suite 3B, New York, New York 10010. Printed in the United States of America.

10 9 8 7 6 5 4 3 2 1

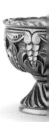

Contents

ANCIENT

Majestic

Proud

Armenia is in southwestern Asia.

It's one of the oldest countries in the world!

Over three million people live there.

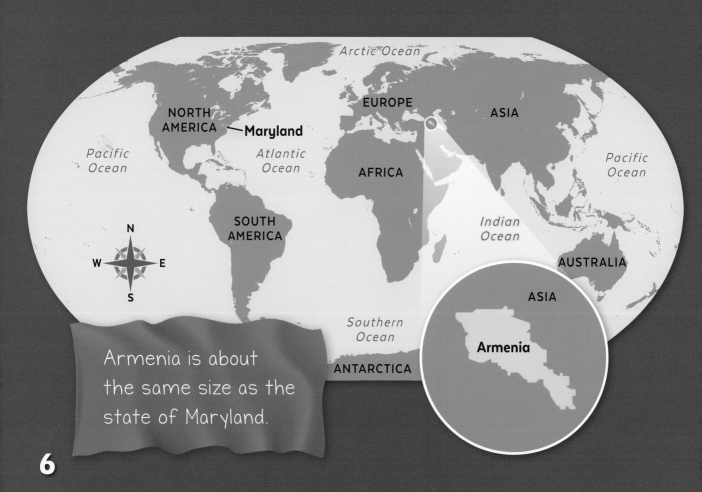

Armenia is about the same size as the state of Maryland.

the Armenian city of Yerevan

Armenia has many mountains, rivers, and lakes.

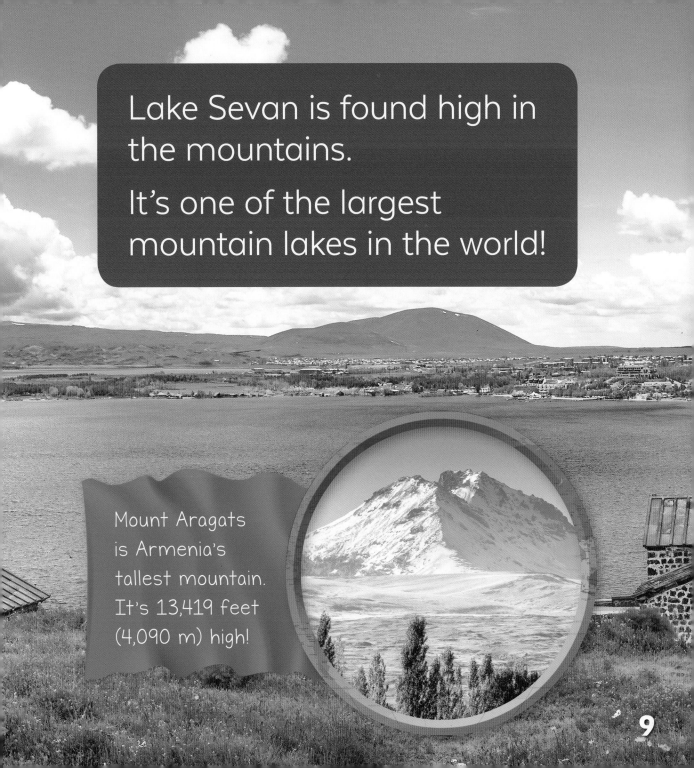

Lake Sevan is found high in the mountains.

It's one of the largest mountain lakes in the world!

Mount Aragats is Armenia's tallest mountain. It's 13,419 feet (4,090 m) high!

9

Many animals live in Armenia.

There are long-eared hedgehogs and slithering snakes.

long-eared hedgehog

rock viper

Mouflons (MOOF-lonz) are big-horned sheep.

They live on rocky mountain cliffs.

Mouflons are **endangered** animals.

11

There are about 375 kinds of birds in Armenia.

Pelicans, gulls, and storks soar through the sky.

The eagle is Armenia's national animal.

Eagles can fly up to 100 miles (161 km) per hour!

Storks often nest on top of telephone poles in Armenia!

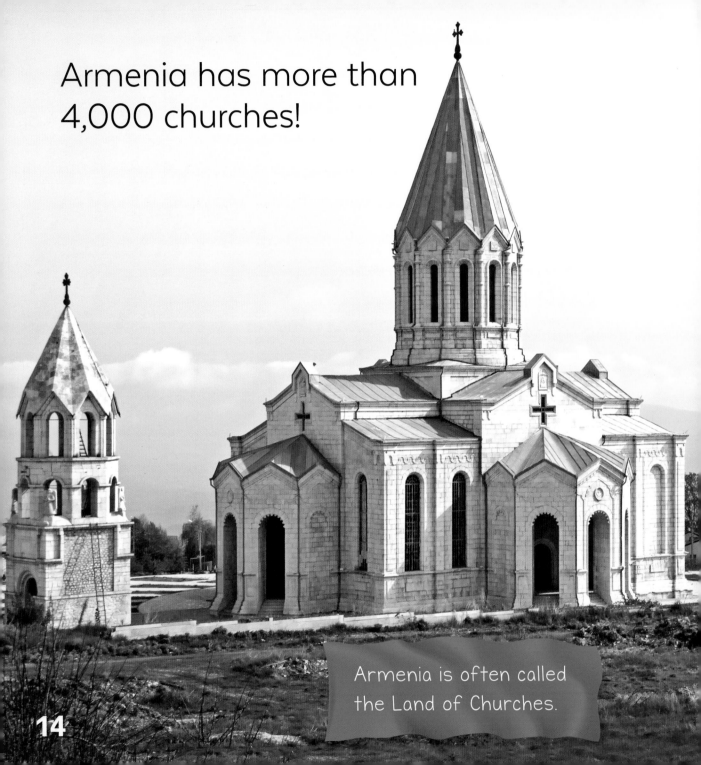

Armenia has more than 4,000 churches!

Armenia is often called the Land of Churches.

14

Echmiadzin **Cathedral** is one of the oldest in the world.

It was built over 1,700 years ago.

Echmiadzin Cathedral

People have lived in Armenia for over 2,500 years.

During that time, different groups were in power.

The Temple of Garni is over 2,000 years old! It was likely built by Tiridates, an Armenian king.

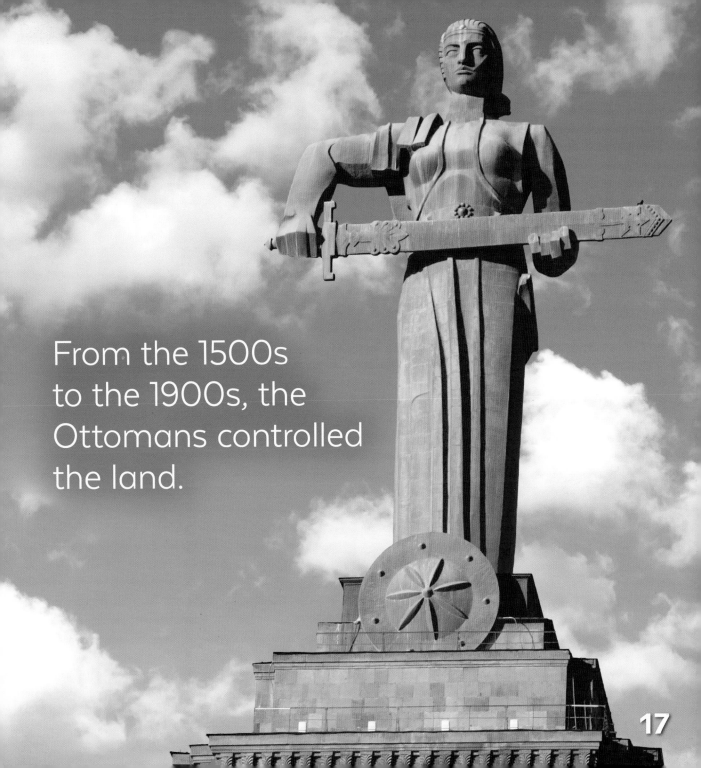

From the 1500s to the 1900s, the Ottomans controlled the land.

In 1915, the Ottomans forced people to leave Armenia.

Over 1.5 million Armenians died as a result.

This is known as the Armenian **Genocide**.

The Armenians built a **memorial** to remember those who died.

the Armenian Genocide memorial

19

Yerevan is the **capital** of Armenia.

It's sometimes called the Pink City.

Many of Yerevan's buildings
are made from pink stone.

Yerevan is home to the world's
first children's art museum.
It holds over 100,000
artworks made by kids!

Bread is very popular in Armenia.

Thin, flat lavash bread is cooked in a *tonir* (tow-NEER).

A tonir is an oven made in the ground.

lavash bread

tonir

Armenians also enjoy eating dolmas, which are stuffed grape leaves.

Apricots have been grown in Armenia for thousands of years!

The main language in Armenia is Armenian.

This is how you say *hello* in Armenian:

Barev (bah-REV)

This is how you say *goodbye*:

Menak parov
(meh-NAK pah-ROV)

There are 38 letters in the Armenian alphabet. There are only 26 letters in the English alphabet.

Armenians love festivals.

One of the most popular is Vardavar (var-duh-VAR).

During Vardavar, people throw water at each other!

It's a way to show love.

Another fun event is the Snow Art Festival. People carve statues out of ice!

Soccer is the most popular sport in Armenia.

People love to play and watch soccer games.

Many Armenians also enjoy skiing on the country's mountains.

Chess is popular, too. Most children are taught how to play the game.

Fast Facts

Capital city: Yerevan

Population of Armenia: Over three million

Main language: Armenian

Money: Armenian dram

Major religion: Christian

Neighboring countries: Azerbaijan, Georgia, Iran, and Turkey

Cool Fact: Armenia has one of the longest tramways in the world! It stretches 18,871 feet (5,752 m)!

Glossary

capital (KAP-uh-tuhl) the city where a country's government is based

cathedral (kuh-THEE-drul) the large, main church in an area

endangered (en-DAYN-jurd) in danger of dying out

genocide (JEN-uh-sayd) the deliberate killing of a large group of people

memorial (muh-MOR-ee-uhl) a structure built to honor something

31

Index

Read More

Dhilawala, Sakina. *Armenia (Cultures of the World).* New York: Cavendish Square (2017).

Hintz, Martin. *Armenia (Enchantment of the World).* New York: Children's Press (2004).

Learn More Online

To learn more about Armenia, visit
www.bearportpublishing.com/CountriesWeComeFrom

About the Author

Rachel Rose lives in San Francisco.
She loves visiting new countries
and is hoping to add Armenia
to her list of places to go.